ABSTRACTS OF PAPERS
READ AT
THE FIRST INTERNATIONAL
EUGENICS CONGRESS

LECTOR HOUSE PUBLIC DOMAIN WORKS

This book is a result of an effort made by Lector House towards making a contribution to the preservation and repair of original classic literature. The original text is in the public domain in the United States of America, and possibly other countries depending upon their specific copyright laws.

In an attempt to preserve, improve and recreate the original content, certain conventional norms with regard to typographical mistakes, hyphenations, punctuations and/or other related subject matters, have been corrected upon our consideration. However, few such imperfections might not have been rectified as they were inherited and preserved from the original content to maintain the authenticity and construct, relevant to the work. We believe that this work holds historical, cultural and/or intellectual importance in the literary works community, therefore despite the oddities, we accounted the work for print as a part of our continuing effort towards preservation of literary work and our contribution towards the development of the society as a whole, driven by our beliefs.

We are grateful to our readers for putting their faith in us and accepting our imperfections with regard to preservation of the historical content. We shall strive hard to meet up to the expectations to improve further to provide an enriching reading experience.

Though, we conduct extensive research in ascertaining the status of copyright before redeveloping a version of the content, in rare cases, a classic work might be incorrectly marked as not-in-copyright. In such cases, if you are the copyright holder, then kindly contact us or write to us, and we shall get back to you with an immediate course of action.

HAPPY READING!

ABSTRACTS OF PAPERS READ AT THE FIRST INTERNATIONAL EUGENICS CONGRESS

UNIVERSITY OF LONDON

ISBN: 978-93-88396-46-2

First Published: -

LECTOR HOUSE LLP
E-MAIL: lectorpublishing@gmail.com

ABSTRACTS OF PAPERS
READ AT
THE FIRST INTERNATIONAL
EUGENICS CONGRESS,

UNIVERSITY OF LONDON.

JULY, 1912.

ENGLISH.

CHARLES KNIGHT & CO., LTD.,
227-239, TOOLEY STREET, LONDON, S.E.

CONTENTS

SECTION II.

PRACTICAL EUGENICS.

SECTION III.

SOCIOLOGY AND EUGENICS.

SECTION IV.

MEDICINE AND EUGENICS.

SECTION I.

BIOLOGY AND EUGENICS.
VARIATION AND HEREDITY IN MAN.

(Abstract.)

BY PROFESSOR G. SERGI,
PROFESSOR OF ANTHROPOLOGY, ROME.

In his paper Professor G. Sergi wishes to show that in man after his morphological characteristics are established there occur no profound variations to change the typical forms which are naturally persistent.

The principal discussion concerns the different forms of the skull which are important as characteristics of race. Professor Sergi distinguishes in the human skull two principal and primordial forms: the dolichomorphic and the brachymorphic are both very ancient, as they are found contemporaneously in European human fossils. Consequently he attacks the idea of the transformation of one form into another. He does not find it demonstrated that the dolichomorphic type is transformed into the brachymorphic, and considers the causes adduced for this supposed transformation insufficient. It is neither the effect of environment of the plains or of the mountains, or the climatic influence of extreme cold, or the increase of volume of the brain supposed to be due to greater cerebral activity owing to a more developed culture, that the form of the skull is transformed into another type. All these suppositions are contrary to facts, because dolichomorphic and brachymorphic skulls are found alike in mountain and plain, in northern and southern regions, among primitive and civilized populations, in fact without any distinction.

The mutations that are believed to be found in the different populations are due to the effect of intermixture and penetration of new demographical elements, and not to the transformation of forms. That is also proved by the crossing of the two different human types from which no intermediary forms are derived: but instead there occurs in the heredity a segregation analagous to that under the Mendelian theory. If this were not so, to-day after many thousands of years of inter-mixture of the most diverse races, there would be but a single form derived from transformation; the demonstration of the facts proves that this has not occurred.

There is a great persistence in human physical forms, the variability is minimum after the formation of the races, and does not effect the changes of type.

The same fact can be noticed for the external characteristics of man, such as the colour of the skin, the colour and form of the hair, and the colour of the iris. It is solely in the crossings that there can be intermediary formations which have not indefinite heredity, because the segregation of characteristics takes place also in this case.

But the studies and observations on this matter are still incomplete, especially according to the Mendelian theory, and there is need of new and careful observation.

As to the pathological inheritance, there exist facts that confirm it in a general way, but the laws under which this heredity occurs have not been fully verified.

ON THE INCREASE OF STATURE IN CERTAIN EUROPEAN POPULATIONS.

(Abstract.)

BY SOREN HANSEN, M.D.,
DIRECTOR OF THE DANISH ANTHROPOLOGICAL SURVEY, CO-PENHAGEN.

The improvement in stature in many European countries during the past 50 years is generally ascribed simply to improved hygienic and economic conditions, but the question is really very intricate. The presence of different racial elements, social selection with its tendency to draw the well-made into towns, and the falling death-rate, etc., complicate the investigations. In all countries there is a great lack of truly comparable data from earlier years. The British Inter-Departmental Committee on Physical Deterioration, for example, though it collected an enormous amount of material, was unsuccessful in its endeavours to solve the main question. Single cases, e.g., the comparison of factory children with the boys of the York Quaker school (Anthropometric Committee, Brit. Ass. 1883), are certainly of great interest, but how can such cases be taken to represent the average?

Other countries possess a rich source of information in their conscription lists. Thus, in Denmark these lists show an unmistakable increase of 3.7 cm. ($1\frac{1}{2}$ inch) in the average height of the adult Dane during the past 50-60 years. Similar increases are noted from Norway, Sweden and Holland. This increase suggests that there may have been more or less periodic waves of increase and decrease in height, since, on the one hand, we cannot imagine such an increase continuing indefinitely, and on the other, we know that the men of, say, 1000 years ago were quite as tall as they are at present. What are the agencies alternately improving or impairing the racial qualities? First of all, have we sufficiently exact, numerical information regarding the racial qualities?

A critical examination of all available data is very necessary. For example, the weight of new-born children is stated to have increased in England by 59 and 82 grams during the past 20 years, and in Denmark we can point to an increase of 40 grams in 35 years. But when we consider all the possible sources of error, it must be admitted that these statements, and especially the former, require confirmation. The material is not homogenous. Again, it is stated, that the average height of adult women in France has increased by 3 cm. in the last 80 years—but when we read that the total number of measurements in the last period was only 255, we cannot rely very much upon this statement.

On the whole, it may be said, that we have a few cases of definite increase and a goodly number very doubtful. We really need to have the first of the principal recommendations of the Inter-Departmental Committee on Physical Deterioration carried out in all countries, for, the more we subject the available data to critical scrutiny, the more we see the hopelessness of attaining to any real and fruitful conclusions, unless we have an efficient organisation of capable workers, backed by governmental as well as private support.

THE SO-CALLED LAWS OF INHERITANCE IN MAN.

(Abstract.)

BY PROFESSOR V. GUIFFRIDA-RUGGERI,
PROFESSOR OF ANTHROPOLOGY, NAPLES.

The Mendelian laws find verification in man. Every race, whether a sub-species or a variety, has an hereditary possession of certain characters; a possession which is completely transmitted to the descendants, in whom is preserved the same germ plasm as in the progenitors.

The researches of C. B. and G. Davenport seem to have proved the recessive character of albinism and its obedience to the Mendelian law. Hurst has presented figures which show that the inheritance of colour in the iris of the human eye obeys Mendelian laws. Davenport has established the order of dominance by the form of hair, which also obeys the Mendelian law.

De Quatrefages, many years before the re-affirmation of Mendel's discoveries, wrote: —

"The union of individuals of different races involves a contest between their two natures—a contest of which the theatre is the field where the new being is organised. Now, this contest does not take place *en bloc*, so to speak, as has been generally admitted. Each of the characters of the two parents struggles on its own account against the corresponding character (its antagonist, as has just been said). When the hereditary energy is equal on both sides there necessarily ensues a kind of process of which the consequence is the fusion of the maternal and paternal characters in an intermediate character. If the energies are very unequal the hybrid inherits a character borrowed entirely from one of his parents; but this parent, conqueror on one point, may be conquered upon another. Hence, there results with the hybrid a *juxtaposition* of characters derived from each of the types of which he is the child."

Above all, I have wished to call attention to the so-called laws of dominance, because of their great importance. We may conclude that in the case of man the dominant characters are also the original ones.

THE INHERITANCE OF FECUNDITY.

(Abstract.)

BY RAYMOND PEARL,
BIOLOGIST, MAINE AGRICULTURAL EXPERIMENT STATION.

The purpose of this paper is to give an account (necessarily abbreviated, and without presentation of complete evidence) of the results of an investigation into the mode of inheritance of fecundity in the domestic fowl, and to point out some of the possible eugenic bearings of these results.

It is shown that while the continued selection, over a period of years, of highly fecund females failed to bring about any change in average fecundity of the strain used, this character must nevertheless be inherited since pedigree lines have been isolated which uniformly breed true to definite degrees of fecundity.

It is further shown that observed variations in actually realized fecundity (number of eggs laid) do not depend upon anatomical differences in respect to the number of visible oöcytes in the ovary. The differential factor on which the variations in fecundity depend must be primarily physiological.

Fecundity in the fowl is shown to be inherited in strict accord with the following Mendelian plan:—

1. Observed individual variations in fecundity depend essentially upon two separately inherited physiological factors (designated L_1, and L_2).

2. *High* fecundity is manifested only when both of these factors are present together in the same individual.

3. Either of these factors when present alone, whether in homozygous or heterozygous form, causes about the same degree of *low* fecundity to be manifested.

4. One of these factors, namely L_2, is sex-limited or sex-correlated in its inheritance, in such way that in gametogenesis any gamete which bears the female sex-determinant F does not bear L_2.

5. There is a definite and clear-cut segregation of high fecundity from low fe-

cundity, in the manner set forth above.

From the standpoint of eugenics it is pointed out that these results furnish a new conception of the mode of inheritance of fecundity, and may be helpful in suggesting a method of attacking the same problem for man.

ETHNIC PSYCHOLOGY AND THE SCIENCE OF EUGENICS.

(Abstract.)

BY PROF. ENRICO MORSELLI,
DIRECTOR OF THE CLINIC FOR MENTAL AND NERVOUS DISEASES, GENOA UNIVERSITY.

All natural varieties or races of mankind differ, not only by their physical, but also by their mental, characters. There exists, therefore, an "Ethnic Psychology" which, along with "Ethnic Somatology," constitutes the complete Science of Anthropology or the Natural History of Man. This must describe and classify races and populations under a double aspect—physical and psychical.

The psychical characters of races are in part *original*, and in part acquired through *adaptation*. These persist in a race as long as such mesological adaptation lasts; they vary with modifications of the conditions of life, including social activities and inter-racial relations.

In mixed unions, amongst different races, there are always some which are more vigorous, biologically and mentally, more fully developed, which impress their characters upon their descendants. For the vitality and well-being of mixed or metamorphic populations a certain amount of difference amongst the parent races is necessary, but too great a difference is injurious to the offspring.

The offspring of mixed unions present in their psychology a *mixture*, again a *combination* or fusion of the mental characters of the parent races: sometimes certain psychical characters of a race become the *dominant* characters.

All ethnic groupings have their destiny marked out by the grade attained in *the human psycho-physical hierarchy.* Nevertheless, it is necessary that each race or nation, when it knows its contribution to the development of universal civilisation, should contemplate the preservation of its own ethnic type. Differentiation amongst peoples is an indispensable factor in human progress.

The science of eugenics should not look for the realisation of a uniform type of man, but vary its aims and methods according to the natural differentiation of races and nations, taking account of ethnic psychology equally with ethnic somatology.

The humanity of the future will be physically and mentally superior to the existing humanity, but the *amelioration of the species* ought not to aim at the equality of races and populations. These races and populations ought not to lose their acquisition of particular adaptations to different conditions of existence.

A science of universal or common eugenics should allow a eugenic ethnology to exist, which should indicate and facilitate for each race or nation the defence and propagation of its own *physical type* and its own *mentality*. The most vigorous and dominant races will always be those which know how to create and preserve in sexual unions their characteristics of structure and culture.

THE INHERITANCE OF EPILEPSY.

(Abstract.)

BY DAVID FAIRCHILD WEEKS, M.D.,
MEDICAL SUPERINTENDENT AND EXECUTIVE OFFICER, THE NEW JERSEY STATE VILLAGE FOR EPILEPTICS AT SKILLMAN, U.S.A.

In this paper the writer has endeavoured to learn what laws, if any, epilepsy follows in its return to successive generations, and the relation it bears to alcoholism, migraine, paralysis, and other symptoms of lack of neural strength.

The data used in the study was analysed according to the Mendelian method which assumes that the inheritance of any character is not from the parents, grandparents, etc., but from the germ plasm out of which every fraternity and its parents and other relatives have arisen. If the soma possesses the trait of the recessive to normality sort, it lacks in its germ plasm the determiner upon which the normal development depends, and this condition is called nulliplex. If the soma possesses the trait of the dominant to normality sort, the determiner was derived from both parents and is double in the germ plasm, or normal, all of the germ cells have the determiner; or else it came from one parent only, is single in the germ plasm, or simplex, and half of the germ cells have and half lack the determiner.

The method of obtaining the data was by means of field workers, who interviewed in their homes the parents, relatives and all others interested in the epileptic patient. These visits have established a friendly feeling toward and an intelligent understanding of the Institution and its work.

The study is based on the data derived from 397 histories, covering 440 matings.

The matings are classified under the six possible types, of nulliplex × nulliplex, nulliplex × simplex, nulliplex × normal, simplex × simplex, simplex × normal, and normal × normal.

Under the first type all those matings where both parents were epileptic, one was epileptic and the other feeble-minded, or both were feeble-minded, are classified. According to Mendel's Law, all of the children should be nulliplex. The data showed all of the children defective.

Under the type nulliplex × simplex, all matings where one parent was epileptic or feeble-minded and the other "tainted," that is, alcoholic, neurotic, migrainous, or showed some mental weakness, are classified. From this type of mating, 50% of the offspring are expected to be nulliplex and 50% simplex. From the matings where one parent was epileptic or feeble-minded and the other alcoholic, there were 61% mentally deficient or nulliplex, the remainder simplex. The figures for the offspring from the other matings showed 47% nulliplex, and 53% simplex.

For the third type, nulliplex by normal, all those matings where one parent was epileptic or feeble-minded and the other reported as mentally normal are classified. From this type of mating, the expectations are that all of the children would be simplex. A study of the ancestors of the normal parents showed these parents simplex rather than normal. The analysis of the offspring showed at least 43% nulliplex, which is a close fitting to the type of mating nulliplex × simplex.

The fourth type of mating is simplex × simplex. Here, all matings where both of the parents were "tainted" are classified. The expectation is that 25% of the offspring would be nulliplex, in reality 35% were found to be mentally deficient.

Simplex × normal is the fifth type of mating considered. The matings where one parent was tainted and the other supposedly normal, are classified here. From a study of their ancestors these normal parents appeared to be simplex, and the classification of the offspring showed more than 25% nulliplex, which is the expectation from simplex × simplex mating.

The sixth type is normal × normal, and the matings where both parents were reported normal is studied under this heading. Here, as before, a study of the ancestors of these normal parents indicates that they are simplex, and not normal. The classification of the children showed a close fitting to the expectation from a simplex × simplex mating.

A special study of the matings where one or both of the parents was migrainous or alcoholic, shows a close relationship between these conditions and epilepsy.

The following conclusions are drawn from the study.

The common types of epileptics lack some element necessary for complete mental development. This is also true of the feeble-minded.

Two epileptic parents produce only defectives. When both parents are either epileptic or feeble-minded their offspring are also mentally defective.

Epilepsy tends in successive generations to form a larger part of the population.

The normal parents of epileptics are not normal but simplex, and have descended from tainted ancestors.

Alcohol may be a cause of defect in that more children of alcoholic parents are defective than where alcoholism is not a factor.

Neurotic and other tainted conditions are closely allied with epilepsy.

In the light of present knowledge, epilepsy, considered by itself, is not a Mendelian factor, but epilepsy and feeble-mindedness are Mendelian factors of the recessive type.

Tainted individuals, as neurotics, alcoholics, criminals, sex offenders, etc., are simplex and normals or simplex and normal in character.

THE INFLUENCE OF THE AGE OF PARENTS ON THE PSY-CHO-PHYSICAL CHARACTERS OF THE OFFSPRING.

(Abstract.)

BY ANTONIO MARRO,
DIRECTOR OF THE LUNATIC ASYLUM, TURIN.

The natural law of heredity holds good whether for the physical characteristics or for those which are biological and moral.

The apparent anomalies which children present in not reproducing the qualities of the parents, and the unlikeness frequently noted among the children of the same family, only serve to reveal the presence of the particular conditions of the parents at the time of begetting which has influenced the offspring.

We have a proof of this law in the anomalies presented by the children of parents who, at the time of begetting, were themselves in anomalous conditions by reason of intoxication or disease.

Among the conditions of parents which are capable of influencing the characteristics of children must be included the changes which their organism undergoes by reason of advancing age.

I propose to study the effects of age on the physical and moral characters of the children. My researches have extended to numerous criminals and insane persons, as well as to scholars of the public schools and other normal persons affected or not with special diseases.

Of my studies on criminals, the result is: that the children of young parents are found in large numbers guilty of offences against property; and this is natural. The first impulse to that is not due to wickedness, which impels them to inflict harm on others, but to love of pleasure, of revel, of idleness—all features of youth, during which period the passions are very active, and no restraint present with which to repress and subjugate them.

Swindlers alone are exceptions to this rule, but swindling is a crime of riper years, according to the dictum of Quetelet.

Among crimes of personal violence, I have found a numerical superiority in the children of aged parents. Assassins, homicides, those who show the completest absence of sentiments of affection and often delusions of persecution more or less pronounced, gave a proportion of children of aged parents far greater than that furnished by all the other categories of delinquents; the proportion is as high for fathers as for mothers of advanced age.

Here, too, we note a certain correlation between the state of discontent, of suspicion, of frigid egoism, which the decline of physical energy tends to arouse in the old, and the absence of affectionate sentiment and a tendency to delusions of persecution which are usual in murderers. Among the insane, moral idiocy in particular, and the degenerative forms in general, appeared more frequently in children of aged parents.

As to schoolboys, I have noticed that the minimum of good conduct and the maximum of better developed intelligence coincides with the possession of youth by both parents.

The age of complete development corresponds to a maximum of good conduct and a minimum of bad conduct, and retains a large proportion of intelligent children.

In the period of decline of both parents, good conduct of children is observed in a smaller proportion than in the preceding period, and high intelligence in a very small proportion.

Among biological qualities I have made observations on longevity; among persons of 70 and 80 whom I have examined there is a large proportion of parents who themselves enjoyed remarkably long lives, which proves the transmissibility from father to son of powers of resistance against the stresses of life.

Among physical qualities I have made note of the fact that from alcoholic or aged parents were descended children in whom degenerative physical characteristics were most frequently apparent, recalling some features of an inferior human type, such as exaggeration of the frontal sinuses, the torus occipitalis, ears with the Darwinian tubercles prominent, the forehead receding, etc. At the same time the ascendants of those who presented typical and anomalous characters, due to morbid influences of various kinds and following on faulty development of the fœtus, such as cretinism, congenital goître, nasal deflections, strabismus, plagio-cephaly, hydrocephaly, dental malformation, etc., showed a large number of alcoholics and epileptics.

The explanation of the pernicious consequences to the psycho-physical characters of the children of parents too young or too advanced in age does not present much difficulty.

At the younger period the organism is still in process of formation; the incomplete development of the skeleton, as of all the other organs, continually absorbs a mass of plastic materials necessary to the formation of offspring. So we may consider that the faults of children born of too young parents are due to an incomplete development because of the insufficiency of plastic material.

We must, on the other hand, seek in the conditions which accompany old age for the reason why it has a disastrous influence on the vitality of the germinal elements of the parents and predisposes the descendants to various forms of physical and moral degeneracy.

During this period we have in the tissues, instead of a development and renewal of protoplasm, the tendency to an accumulation of fat; and in the whole organism, chiefly in the tissues of the arterial system, we find the tendency to a deposit in their structure of an amorphous substance which converts the supple elastic canals into rigid tubes; and from this a general slowing up of the organic functions (circulation, oxidation, secretion) results; the blood, not reaching the degree of elaboration which it possessed before, acquires a greater acidity, and cannot by the ordinary excretory channels so quickly get rid of the catabolic products with which it is charged.

By reason of these conditions the organism of older people undergoes a sort of slow and gradual intoxication, which, at the same time as it shows itself in the individual by the gradual languishing of all his functions, influences in a disastrous manner the germs which develop within him, and predisposes them to become beings condemned to degeneracy.

Consequently this cause of degeneracy enters the general category of intoxications.

GENETICS AND EUGENICS.

(Abstract.)

BY R. C. PUNNETT,
PROFESSOR OF BIOLOGY, CAMBRIDGE.

To the student of genetics, man, like any other animal, is material for working out the manner in which characters, whether physical or mental, are transmitted from one generation to the next. Viewed in this way he must be regarded as unpromising, not only from the small size of his families, the time consumed in their production, and the long period of immaturity, but also because full experimental control is here out of the question. For these reasons man is of interest to the student of genetics, chiefly in so far as he presents problems in heredity which are rarely to be found in other species, and can only be studied at present in man himself. The aim of the Eugenist, on the other hand, is to control human mating in order to obtain the largest proportion of individuals he considers best fitted to the form of society which he affects. It is evident that to do this effectually he must have precise knowledge of the manner in which transmission of characters occurs, and more especially of those with which he particularly wishes to deal. Precise knowledge is at present available in man for relatively few characters; and those characters, such as eye-colour, and certain somewhat rare deformities, are not the kind on which the Eugenist lays great stress. The one instance of eugenic importance that could be brought under immediate control is that of feeble-mindedness. Speaking generally, the available evidence suggests that it is a case of simple Mendelian inheritance. Occasional exceptions occur, but there is every reason to expect that a policy of strict segregation would rapidly bring about the elimination of this character.

There is reason to suppose that many human qualities are more complicated in their transmission, and it is probable that certain phenomena now being studied in plants and animals will throw definite light upon man. Though characters are frequently transmitted on the Mendelian scheme quite independently of one another, there are cases known in which they are linked up more or less completely in the germ cells with the determinant of a particular sex. Sex-limited inheritance of this nature has been carefully worked out in particular cases in Lepidoptera and poultry. As yet there is much to be learnt in this direction, and further progress may be expected to lead eventually to a precise knowledge of the mode of transmission of many human defects, such as colour-blindness and hæmophilia. It is not unlikely that a similar mode of transmission will be found to hold good for many human characters usually classed as normal.

Another set of phenomena which will probably be found of importance in the heredity of man are those included under the terms "coupling" and "repulsion." Characters, each exhibiting simple Mendelian segregation, may become linked together more or less completely in the process of heredity, or the reverse may occur. Our knowledge of these phenomena is at present almost completely confined to cases in plants, but evidence is beginning to be obtained for their occurrence in animals. It is not unlikely that they will be found to play a considerable part in human heredity. For one of the most noticeable things about man is the frequency with which children resemble one or other parent to the seemingly almost complete exclusion of the other. In view of the mongrelisation of the human race, the frequency of these cases is very remarkable, and can hardly fail to suggest that some sort of coupling between characters plays a large part in human heredity.

Except in very few cases, our knowledge of heredity in man is at present far too slight and too uncertain to base legislation upon. On the other hand, experience derived from plants and animals has shewn that problems of considerable complexity can be unravelled by the experimental method, and the characters concerned brought under control. Though the direct method is hardly feasible in man, much may yet be learnt by collecting accurate pedigrees and comparing them with standard cases worked out in other animals. But it must be clearly recognised that the collection of such pedigrees is an arduous undertaking demanding high critical ability, and only to be carried out satisfactorily by those who have been trained in and are alive to the trend of genetic research.

SECTION II.

PRACTICAL EUGENICS.

GENERAL CONSIDERATIONS UPON "EDUCATION BEFORE PROCREATION."

(Abstract.)

BY ADOLPHE PINARD,
PROFESSOR AT THE FACULTY; MEMBER OF THE ACADEMY OF MEDICINE OF PARIS.

Sir Francis Galton has entitled Eugenics the new science having for its object the study of the causes subject to social control which can improve or impair the racial qualities of future generations, whether physical or mental.

Eugenics, thus defined, is nothing else but "Education before Procreation," which has been studied in France for a number of years, and which constitutes the first part of child-culture, "a science having for its object the search for information relative to the reproduction, preservation, and improvement of the human species"([1]).

The Congress ought then to have for its object to work for the investigation of the conditions necessary to secure a favourable procreation. Now, it appears that the word "Eugenics," from the etymological point of view, does not characterise either explicitly or sufficiently the proposed object, while the word "Eugénique," of [Greek: gennaô], at once recalls to the mind the idea of a favourable procreation([2]).

It is part of the duty of our first principal sitting to lay down a rule upon this point.

---

[1] v. De la Puériculture in Revue Scientifique, 1897.
[2] Besides, the word "Eugenics" recalls in France a chemical term: eugenic-acid.

Certainly, biological, sociological, and historical researches, laws and social customs regarded in their relations with the science of Eugenics, are necessary and will undoubtedly result in extremely interesting data, but from now it is above all things urgent to establish and proclaim eugenic principles.

Researches relating to physiological heredity and pathological heredity ought to be pursued without interruption, but it is necessary to make known as soon as possible to the masses of the people the individual conditions, fully understood, which alone permit a favourable and healthy procreation. In a word, it is necessary, by every means and as soon as possible, to organise a great movement in order to show to the greatest number of human beings the absolute necessity for a conscientious, *i.e.,* an enlightened procreation. We must bravely approach the civilising of *the reproductive instinct*, which alone has remained in a barbarous state amongst all the so-called civilised nations from the earliest times.

Then only, when societies have fulfilled this duty, will they have the right to investigate what they ought and can effect against those for whom future offspring would be recognised as fatally disastrous.

Finally, it is fully understood that researches relating to selection in the human species must be pursued in a parallel manner, as is now done with such fruitful results for animals and vegetables in Genetics, and in throwing light upon the constantly increasing conquests of this other science.

PRACTICAL ORGANIZATION OF EUGENIC ACTION.

(Abstract.)

BY DR. LOUIS QUERTON,
PROFESSOR AT THE UNIVERSITY OF BRUSSELS.

Now that many studies on the physiology and hygiene of reproduction of man have been made, and many investigations on degeneration have been conducted, we may face the problem of the betterment of the race, from a practical standpoint.

If the eugenic action cannot yet strive directly against hereditary transmission of anomalies, it can fight successfully against the causes of degeneration which act during the development of the individual.

Physical and social environment influences these causes, which, on account of their growing complexity, create more and more obstacles to the normal evolution of the individual, while at the same time they force him to acquire greater and more varied aptitudes.

To thwart the prejudicial action of the environment on the development of the individual, the systematic organization of this development seems to be of first importance.

The control of the development of the children, at the different phases of their evolution, is strictly necessary to assure the education of the individual and to check the degeneration of the race.

The control is already established for certain classes of children, and during limited periods of their development. Nurslings, school children, and labourers can already, sometimes compulsorily, be submitted to control.

But the insufficiency of the actual organization is very evident, and the results are, from the eugenic standpoint, unsatisfactory.

In order to be really effective and to contribute to the improvement of the individual and to the betterment of the race, the control of the development should, as far as possible, be exerted over all children, and it should last during the whole period of their evolution. This control should be compulsory, as well as education; it should be exercised by an institution, the frequentation of which, as well as that of school, might be forced upon all children whose development is not submitted to an effective control in their homes. Private initiative should create such institutions everywhere, and thus prepare legislative interference.

These methodically organized eugenic institutions should, in the future, be the development of the administrative institutions, which actually establish the civil state of individuals. They would tend to facilitate the education of individuals and public bodies; at the same time they would assure the strict application of the laws concerning the protection and education of childhood.

They would collect the documents necessary to the scientific knowledge of the facts of heredity, and would supply precise information concerning the effective work of different social institutions on transformation of the race.

MARRIAGE LAWS AND CUSTOMS.

(Abstract.)

BY C. B. DAVENPORT,
DIRECTOR, EUGENICS RECORD OFFICE, U.S.A.

Of the various laws limiting freedom of marriage three are of biological import. First, the limitation of relationship between the mates; second, the limitations in mental capacity of the mates; and third, limitations of race.

For the first there is a biological justification in so far as cousin marriages are apt to bring in from both sides of the house the same defect. For the second the justification is partial; but there is equal reason for forbidding the marriage of normal persons both of whom have mentally defective parents or other close relatives. The denial of marriage between races has this justification, that most other races have not, through selection, attained the social status of the Caucasian. In such cases the socially inadequate should be sterilized or segregated in other races as well as in the Caucasian.

EUGENIC SELECTION AND THE ORIGIN OF DEFECTS.

(Abstract.)

BY FRÉDÉRIC HOUSSAY,
PROFESSOR OF SCIENCE, UNIVERSITY OF PARIS.

Eugenics, which is a social application of biological science, cannot yet be judged by its results; it must be judged by its tendencies. To determine these, we must adjust them to principles generally admitted.

And inasmuch as it advocates practical rules and seeks to check the propagation of the unfit, by isolation or sterilization (voluntary or enforced), it is an artificial selection.

Its justification lies in the fact that, without intervention, the descendants of defectives or degenerates would, in a few generations, eliminate themselves by early death of children or by natural sterility. This would produce a natural selection which Eugenics simply proposes to anticipate by social economy.

It seems that, by applying Darwinian principles, the group of defectives, considered at a given moment, could be rapidly extinguished. But this group is continually reinforced by fresh degeneration of healthy stocks which become tainted.

Hence the need to keep our eye on the re-formation of the group as well as its elimination, and to keep in touch with Lamarckian principles. The study of the origin and hereditary conservation of defects points already as essential factors, to alcoholism, syphilis, and more generally every chronic ailment and diathesis, among which gout must be put in a leading position. Everything which will tend to restrain the action of these factors is of capital importance from our present point of view, whether it occurs in the ranks of rich or poor.

The questions, thus, which Eugenics seeks to answer would be on this view reduced to questions of hygiene and morals.

So that the different biological principles, which sometimes seem in mutual opposition, would become convergent, and would find in Eugenics a ready reconciliation and a field of useful co-operation.

PRELIMINARY REPORT TO THE FIRST INTERNATIONAL EUGENICS CONGRESS,OF THE COMMITTEE OF THE EUGENICS SECTION OF THE AMERICAN BREEDERS' ASSOCIATION TO STUDY AND REPORT ON THE BEST PRACTICAL MEANS FOR CUTTING OFF THE DEFECTIVE GERM PLASM IN THE HUMAN POPULATION.

(Abstract.)

BY BLEECKER VAN WAGENEN,
CHAIRMAN.

1. Brief history of the American Breeders' Association, the Eugenics Section and the Committee on Elimination of Defective Germ Plasm.

2. Concise statement of the problem before the Committee and reasons for the investigation.

3. History of legislation in the United States authorising or requiring the sterilization of certain classes of criminals, defectives and degenerates who are under the control of the State in institutions. Digest of the laws now in force. (This may be given as a lantern slide with greater effect.)

Legal views concerning the constitutionality of these laws.

4. Investigations of vasectomy in Indiana, Illinois, Massachusetts and elsewhere, with detailed reports of some typical cases. (With lantern slides.)

5. Reports of sterilization of females, both of normal and abnormal mentality, with a number of typical cases showing after-effects. (With lantern slides.)

6. Some observations in thremmatology suggesting important questions concerning the practical effectiveness of sterilization as a eugenic measure.

7. Technical description of several kinds of sterilizing operations as now performed. Vasectomy, ovariotomy and salpingectomy (with and without complete excision), castration.

8. Reports of several cases of persons, male and female, who having been completely sterilized for a time, recovered the power of procreation and actually did procreate thereafter.

9. State of public opinion regarding sterilization in the United States at the present time. Letters from Governors of States, views of Social Workers and Institution people. Conflicting views of Roman Catholics (as such). Digest of arguments set forth in a long controversy carried on in the American Ecclesiastical Review, chiefly in Latin.

10. Brief report of other data collected by the Committee and programme for future work, with a call for co-operation in securing further data pertinent to this inquiry.

EUGENICS AND THE NEW SOCIAL CONSCIOUSNESS.

(Abstract.)

BY SAMUEL GEORGE SMITH.

The new social consciousness is indicated; first, by the larger powers and duties assumed by the State: second, by the new sense of social solidarity affecting persons and groups of persons within the State. The exclusion from parenthood of such wards of the State as the feeble-minded, the insane, and the pauper has gone beyond debate; and for all that are legally excluded from parenthood, custodial care is required. There is need to develop a new ethical sense of the individual in regard to his own relations to the social group. We have not yet sufficient facts to establish a definite relation between physical fitness and social efficiency. This is the place for caution.

Questions of maternity among the poor: (*a*) Hard labour must be forbidden to the expectant mother; (*b*) she must have nourishing food; (*c*) surroundings must be wholesome. The economic problem is solved in the increased vitality and consequent earning power of the coming generation.

Problem of the parenthood of the better classes: just as important and more difficult. The question is not only vital and economic; it is also ethical.

The ignorance of parents and the defects of children. The State has invaded the home, and has set standards, both physical and moral, for the family. It is the duty of the State to secure the proper physical environment for the home. It is a municipal problem. It is a problem of public health. The whole movement looks to the triumph of a vital democracy, which is more important than either political or industrial democracy.

Relations of alcoholism to neurasthenia, of tuberculosis to feeble-mindedness, of bad social and labour conditions to both, indicate cross sections in the problem. Vices of the rich in most countries are greater than the vices of the poor. A vital democracy cannot be based upon physical tests and material comfort. Its deepest foundations are psychical and ethical.

PRACTICABLE EUGENICS IN EDUCATION.

(Abstract.)

BY DR. F. C. S. SCHILLER.

The danger to mankind arising from the preservation of the unfit under social conditions. The self-destructiveness of civilization. Its superiority dependent on the transmission of accumulated knowledge by education. The danger of failure in educational systems. Is the education of the rich necessarily a failure? The middle classes as providers of ability to man the professions; but the price they have to pay at present is too often racial extinction. The draining of ability from the lower classes.

The existing educational system and its potential value for eugenics. Its unintellectual character. The liberal endowment of a "liberal education." Commercialism and the scholarship system. The athletic system, the play instincts and moral training. Both systems are Darwinian and appeal to British character.

Suggested improvements: (1) in the athletic system; "fitness," not a merely physical ideal; (2) in the scholarship system; "liberal education" to be conceived as intrinsically useful, and not merely a game with intrinsically useless subjects.

Should scholarships be restricted to the needy? The educational dangers of this policy. The eugenical value of the existing system.

The possibility of infusing eugenical spirit into athletics. The appeal of eugenics to the upper classes. A real versus a sham nobility. The eugenical ideal essentially a matter of sentiment and not necessarily anti-democratic.

SECTION III.

Sociology and Eugenics.
THE PSYCHO-PHYSICAL ELITE AND THE ECONOMIC ELITE.

(Abstract.)

BY PROFESSOR ACHILLE LORIA,
UNIVERSITY OF TURIN.

Artificial selection could be perfectly applied to the human species, in which case marriages would be arranged between persons better endowed, physically and mentally, and the worse endowed would be excluded from marriage. But this selection encounters the gravest practical difficulties; because, if it is relatively easy to estimate the physical qualities of man, nothing on the other hand is harder than to estimate his mental qualities. A dynamometer of intelligence does not exist, and Galton's method of observing the points of merit of University graduates is very insufficient and fallible.

In face of these difficulties there naturally arises the idea of inferring the psycho-physical aptitudes of individuals from their social and economic position, or from their income, which is easily measured. In accord with this idea, it would be a question of acting so that marriages would be effected exclusively and predominantly amongst individuals provided with superior incomes, and to prevent, as far as possible, marriages between persons of inferior incomes, or of no income at all.

But all this would be plausible if there should be a real analogy between the economic élite, and the psycho-physical élite, or if the former were really a product of the latter. Now, this is precisely what I deny. The *economic élite* is not in the least the product of the possession of superior qualities, but is simply the result of a blind struggle between incomes, which carries to the top those who, at the start, possess a larger income through causes which may be absolutely independent of the possession of superior endowments. (See my *Sintesi economica*—Paris, Giard et

Briard, 1911.) Hence, nothing makes it impossible that the wealthier people should be precisely the worst endowed, physically and mentally, and this as a matter of fact happens in innumerable cases.

Besides, we have an indirect proof of this in the very results of selective processes as, until now, they are practised. And, in fact, conjugal selection to-day takes place precisely amongst individuals of the same class, or belonging to the same standard of income, so that persons of the upper classes always marry exclusively amongst each other. So then these marriages, which, according to the theory, ought to give more splendid results, give, on the contrary, more wretched results. Galton's same law of "return to the mean," or the fact that the descendants of persons of high class sometimes have inferior endowments as compared with the average of the race, could not be fulfilled if persons of the upper classes who marry with each other were really select persons, physically and mentally.

There would also be in this case a falling off from the super-normal qualities of an exceptionally gifted parent, but in that case the characters of the children would always be superior to those of the descendants of the lower classes. If this does not happen, if the children of the upper classes show qualities inferior to those of the average of children of the lower classes, this proves conclusively that married people of the superior classes were not in the least endowed with specially high aptitudes, but, on the contrary, presented the opposite characteristics. Thus, the same law of Galton, properly interpreted, shows the absolute independence of largeness of income and excellence of individual qualities, hence the absurdity and danger of Eugenics upon an economic foundation, such as many desire.

The researches of Fahlbeck upon the Swedish nobility, which show the rapid extinction of the upper classes who practise *Economic Eugenics*, is a further proof of the absence of any link between economic superiority and psycho-physical superiority; since if the wealthier people, who usually intermarry, were really the better endowed, their descendants would never show those phenomena of extinction which betray a leaven of inner degeneration.

I conclude that Economic Eugenics is already practised to-day upon a large scale, and hence it is already possible to form an accurate judgment upon its results—which are those of return to the mean—degeneration and extinction of race. Now, these same results show that the economically superior classes are not at all the best endowed, and often even degenerate, and that, therefore, the only method calculated to effect a conjugal selection which would be socially useful is not to unite in marriage the richer people, but individuals really possessing superior qualities, and to exclude from marriage those who do not possess them.

THE CAUSE OF THE INFERIORITY OF PHYSICAL AND MENTAL CHARACTERS IN THE LOWER SOCIAL CLASSES.

(Abstract.)

BY PROFESSOR ALFREDO NICEFORO,
OF THE UNIVERSITY OF NAPLES.

The author has compared the physical, demographic, and mental characters of the upper and leisured classes with the same characters in individuals of the inferior and poor classes. He has made use of several methods: (1) A comparison between the well-to-do and the poor children in schools; (2) a comparison between individuals belonging to different professions; (3) a comparison between the rich and the poor quarters of the same city.

He has also studied 4,000 children of the schools of Lausanne; Italian peasants; conscripts of different countries, classified according to their occupation; and the rich and the poor quarters of Lausanne, Paris, etc.

He has found that individuals of the lower classes show a smaller development of stature, of cranial capacity, of sensibility, of resistance to mental fatigue, a delay in the period when puberty makes its appearance, a slackening in growth, a very large number of anomalies, etc.

The causes of these differences ascertained in comparing the two groups are of the *mesological* and *individual order*.

Of the *mesological* order because the conditions of life where men of the lower classes are forced to live constitute one of the causes of the deterioration of their physical and mental characters.

Of the *individual* order because, thanks to biological variation, every man is born different from all other men, and men who are born with superior physical and mental characters tend to rise in the superior classes, while men who are born with inferior physical and mental characters tend to fall in the most wretched classes.

However, in studying the catalogues of measurements and observations, the author has found that in the mass of men belonging to the superior classes one finds a small number of men with inferior qualities, while in the mass of men forming the inferior classes one finds a certain number of men presenting superior characters.

It is between these two *exceptional* categories that social exchanges should be made, allowing the best and most capable of the lower stratum to ascend, and compelling the unadapted who are found above to fall to the lower stratum.

THE FERTILITY OF MARRIAGES ACCORDING TO PROFESSION AND SOCIAL POSITION.

(Abstract.)

BY M. LUCIEN MARCH,
DIRECTEUR DE LA STATISTIQUE GÉNÉRALE DE LA FRANCE.

Statistics of families furnish, perhaps, the most appropriate data for the examination of the factors which govern the productiveness of marriages or their sterility.

Statistics concerning the children born in the eleven and a half million French families, classed according to occupation, have been prepared in France for the first time as a result of the census of 1906. These statistics give information as to the number of children per family, either alive on the day of the census or previously deceased, in each occupation, for all the families in the whole country taken together, and for the different provinces. Further, a special investigation of the 200,000 families of employees and workmen in the public services has furnished more circumstantial details, which have enabled the number of children and number of deaths of children in a family to be brought into relation with the income of the head.

The results obtained by the method described above are the subject of this report. The effects of occupation, social position and income are analysed by means of co-efficients expressing the productiveness of marriages, after eliminating the influence of such factors as duration of marriage, age, and habitat, all of which may obviously affect the productiveness of a marriage.

These results confirm what has been learnt from previous researches of the fertility of different social classes, but they go further in that they show that the difference is not exclusively dependent on income.

In general there are more children per family in the families of workmen than in the families of employers, and the latter contain more than those of employees other than workmen. Further, one finds industries in which the number of children in the employers' families is larger than in the families of workmen in other industries. Thus, differences are introduced by the occupation. Industries employing many hands seem the more favourable to the production of large families, both among workmen and among employers. Agriculture, in which a large number of persons are engaged in France, does not seem to conduce to fertility.

Fishermen and sailors in the merchant service, on the other hand, appear to form the class in which fertility is the most considerable.

The importance of the occupational factor is such that we could place its influence on the same plane as that of "concentration" of population, with which it is in close relation, since persons following certain classes of occupation, as, for instance, the members of the liberal professions, and clerks and other salaried employees are most numerous in towns.

It does not appear that in France casual and unskilled labourers, persons in the receipt of Poor Law relief, etc., are specially prolific. There is not thus in reality too much risk of seeing the renewal of the population carried out in a dangerous manner by its least valuable section. However, even among the working classes, the most highly paid occupations are not those among which one finds the greatest number of children.

The economic, social, or moral burden of children is a factor bound up in a complex manner, not only with the individual conditions of existence, but also with the transformations of society, progress in manners and customs, and the conception which one forms of life.

It is this burden which must be allieviated where allievation would be most effective and produce the best results, in order to put a stop to a movement which may be dangerous to civilisation.

EUGENICS AND MILITARISM.

(Abstract.)

BY VERNON L. KELLOGG.
(PROFESSOR IN STANFORD UNIVERSITY, CALIFORNIA.)

The claim that war and military service have a directly deteriorating influence through military selection on a population much given to militarism, has been clearly stated by von Liebig, Karl Marx, Herbert Spencer, Tschouriloff, Otto Seeck, David Starr Jordan, and others, not to mention the ever-anticipating Greeks. Military selection may be conceived to work disastrously on a population both through the actual killing during war by wounds and disease of the sturdy young men selected by conscription or recruiting, and also by the removal from the reproducing part of the population of much larger numbers of these selected young men both in war and peace times. Another phase of the racial danger from military service is the possibility of the contraction of persistent and heritable disease which may be carried back from camp and garrison with the return of the soldiers to the population at home.

As likely as seem all these and certain other anti-eugenic influences arising from military selection, the substantiation of their actual results on a basis of observed facts is necessary to give them real standing as eugenic arguments against militarism.

The writer is engaged at present in an attempt to find and expose certain actual results of military service and war that have direct relation to racial modification. His paper presents some pertinent facts and figures already gained. These facts are examined in the light of the criticisms of such men as Bischoff and Livi, who have recognized the weaknesses in military and hygienic statistics, and in the light of other opportunities for error both in the recording and the interpretation of the facts, which have suggested themselves to him. Also there has to be considered the possible reality of eugenic advantages from military selection. Seeck and Ammon believe they have discovered some.

The writer, holding in mind both the dangers of error and the possibility of eugenic advantage, believes himself nevertheless able to present certain definite facts showing considerable direct eugenic disadvantage in certain types of militarism.

EUGENICS IN PARTY ORGANIZATION.

(Abstract.)

BY ROBERTO MICHELS,
UNIVERSITY OF TURIN, ITALY.

An oligarchy is invariably formed in all political parties for reasons based partly on individual psychology, partly on crowd psychology, and partly on the social necessity of party organisation. Under the first head is grouped the individual's consciousness of his own importance, which with opportunity develops into the natural human lust for power, and, further, such individual qualities as native tact, editorial ability, and so on. Crowd psychology is characterised chiefly by the incompetence of the masses, their dependence upon traditional methods of party government, and their feeling of gratitude to leaders who have suffered for the cause. Finally, the necessity for party organisations grows with every increase of numbers and extension of functions. It is physically impossible for large party groups to govern themselves directly. All parties live in a state of perpetual warfare with opposing parties, and, if they are revolutionary in character, with the social order itself. Tactical considerations, therefore, and, above all, the necessity of maintaining a condition of military preparedness, strengthen the hands of the controlling clique within the party and render every day more impossible genuine democracy.

The selective or eugenic value of party organization is that it allows men gifted with certain qualities to rise above their fellows into positions of superiority, which, for the considerations set forth above, are more or less permanent. This value is of the greater importance because the opportunities for able and ambitious workmen to rise by the economic ladder to the rank of employers are rapidly disappearing, at any rate, in old countries.

The qualities necessary for a successful party leader are discussed. Briefly stated, they consist of oratorical ability, which is partly a psychical and partly a physiological and anatomical character; energy of will; superiority of intellect and knowledge; a depth of conviction often bordering on fanaticism and self-confidence, pushed even to the point of self-conceit. Also in many countries, as for instance Italy, physical beauty is important in helping a man to rise, while in rarer cases goodness of heart and disinterestedness influence the crowd by reawakening religious sentiments.

We have seen that some elements of the crowd are seized by the selecting-machine of the party organisation that raises them above their companions, increasing automatically the social distance between them and their followers. To put this automatical selecting-machine into action, certain individuals appear, possessing special physical and intellectual gifts that distinguish them spontaneously from the mass of the party.

THE INFLUENCE OF RACE ON HISTORY.

(Abstract.)

BY W. C. D. AND C. D. WHETHAM.

The history of Europe presents a long series of nations successively rising and falling in the scale of prosperity and influence. Such persistent alternations suggest a common cause underlying the phenomena. All history is the record of change. The outward change as recorded by the chronicler has probably its counterpart in unnoticed variations of the internal biological structure of the nation.

Most nations are composite in character. They contain two or more racial stocks, fulfilling different functions in the national life. It is probable that the proportion in which these stocks are present is not always constant. The variation in proportion is possibly the agent effecting the internal change in structure, which becomes manifest outwardly in the rise or decline of the nation.

The physical characters of the population of Europe during historic times indicate three chief races: (1) the Mediterranean, (2) the Alpine, (3) the Northern. The individuals of these races possess also distinct mental and intellectual attributes, and the history of Europe is fundamentally the story of the interaction of the three races.

It is suggested that the supreme power of Greece and Rome, each in its own direction, was due to the attainment of a fortunate balance between the social and political functions of the constituents of the nation, the directing power being supplied chiefly by the invaders of northern race, who formed the dominant class among the southern indigenous Mediterranean population. In each case, the northern elements grew gradually less, through such agencies as losses in war, the selective action of a differential birth rate, and by racial merging into the more numerous southern stock.

The outburst of artistic genius and intellectual pre-eminence which marked the Renaissance in North Italy may perhaps be due to a similar racial composition, the northern elements being supplied by the descendants of the barbarian invaders of the later Roman Empire.

Great Britain has also similar racial elements. The Mediterranean race, spreading up the shores of the Atlantic, enters largely into the composition of the people of the south-west. The northern element, immigrant from the shores of the Baltic and North Sea, is strongest in the east and north.

We know that there are now at work two influences affecting the average racial character of the English nation; (1) the increase in the urban population at the expense of the rural, (2) the voluntary restriction of the birth rate which affects certain sections of all classes more than others. It is probable that both these changes tend to favour selectively the southern racial elements at the expense of the northern. Eventually, the present structure of society may become unstable in consequence of this racial alteration, and the necessary readjustment, in its turn, will contribute a chapter to history.

SOME INTER-RELATIONS BETWEEN EUGENICS AND HISTORICAL RESEARCH.

(Abstract.)

BY FREDERICK ADAMS WOODS, M.D.,
HARVARD MEDICAL SCHOOL.

The relative influence of heredity and environment has long been a subject for debate, but, for the most part, such debates have not been profitable. It is true that heredity cannot be separated from environment if only one individual be considered; but as soon as we inquire into the causes of the differences between man and man, it is perfectly possible to gain real light on this subject, so important to the advocates of eugenics. Everything must be made a problem of differences. The mathematical measurements of resemblances between relatives close of kin will sometimes serve. At other times, the correlation co-efficient is of no avail, and only an intensive study of detailed pedigrees will bring out such differences as cannot be due to the action of surroundings.

History and genealogy both speak unmistakably for heredity. Men of genius have as many eminent relationships as the expectations of heredity demand. The same is true among the highest aristocratic classes, and is equally true under democratic government, as is proved by a study of the family history of those Americans whose names are in the Hall of Fame. History shows that about half of the early monarchs were not cruel or were not licentious. Alternative heredity can well account for that. Virtuous types have only slightly increased in numerical proportion. Environment cannot be very effective; but there are biological factors of a more hidden nature which are silently making for progress. Mental qualities are correlated with moral; and in the European dynasties the survivors have been generally the descendants of the morally superior.

Physical differences can also be demonstrated, coming in the course of generations. A study of the portraits of royal, noble, and other historical personages shows that the bony framework of the face, especially about the nose and eyes, has changed rapidly since the beginning of the sixteenth century.

In explaining the rise and fall of nations, gametic and personal causes can be measured and marked. All the evidence of history points to the power and importance of a very few great personalities—they themselves the product of inborn forces. These have been the chief causes of political and economic differences, but non-gametic (environmental) causation can be occasionally detected, and separated out; as, for instance, the modern scientific productivity in Germany and the proportionate intellectual activity among women in America. It is estimated that there are four hundred thousand books on history. These form an almost un-worked mine of information, easily available to every student of eugenics. It is high time that the human record, so ancient in its beginnings, should be used to contribute to that most modern of sciences, the improvement of the human breed.

DEMOGRAPHICAL CONTRIBUTIONS TO THE PROBLEMS OF EUGENICS.

(Abstract.)

BY DR. CORRADO GINI,
PROFESSOR OF STATISTICS IN THE ROYAL UNIVERSITY OF CAGLIARI, ITALY.

Tables of mortality relating to human beings with classification as to age, when compared with similar statistics relating to the equine species, show that man during the period of development has a much heavier death-rate. It is not possible to say whether in their natural state the higher kinds of animals possess a higher or lower death-rate during the period of development than when under domestication, but the second of the alternatives seems more likely. It remains to be determined whether the heavy death-rate during development which the human race shows in the comparison is a distinctive natural characteristic belonging to it, or whether it is rather the result of the more or less artificial circumstances in which man is born and reared.

The human race differs as regards reproduction and the rearing of its offspring from the higher species of animals in their natural state, chiefly in three ways: (*a*) In the case of the human race reproduction takes place at all times of the year, whilst the higher animals have one single period for reproducing, or, in some cases, two or three periods; (*b*) animals reproduce as soon as the organism becomes capable of reproduction, whilst in civilised human races as a rule a longer or shorter period elapses between the time when the individual becomes capable of reproduction and the time he actually begins to reproduce; (*c*) in civilised man the development of altruistic sentiments protects weak and sickly persons from the eliminating action of natural selection, and often enables them to take part in the procreation of future generations.

The paper of A. has for its object to examine closely these three arguments based upon very extensive data taken partly from demographic statistics and partly from researches made personally by him or which he caused to be made, especially in the Municipal Statistical Offices of Rome and Cagliari, and in the Obstetrical Clinic of Bologna. The principal results are here indicated.

A. The rule of a greater number of conceptions in Spring observed in temperate regions suffers notable exceptions in tropical and arctic regions. Hence there is a weakening of the idea that in it one should recognise the atavistic heritage of a special season for reproduction which the human race had originally shown, analogous to what one finds to-day in many species of animals. On the other hand, neither the frequency of multiple births, of miscarriages, or of stillbirths, nor the length of life of offspring nor their intellectual capacity show any correlation whatever with the season of conception. The frequency of stillbirths, however, and the length of life of the offspring show a clear correlation with the season of birth, in the sense that those born in temperate seasons show a lower rate for stillbirths and a greater length of life.

B. The age of the mother at the time of parturition does not show any regular influence on the size and weight of the child. It has a very sensible influence on the frequency of miscarriages and of stillbirths; this increases with the increase in age. The age of the mother at the time of marriage exercises a decisive influence upon the vitality of the offspring: the greater the age of the mother at the time of marriage the less will be the vitality of the children.

The age of the father at the birth of his child has some influence on the number of stillbirths among his children. This influence—at any rate above a given age—increases with the increase in the father's age. It can neither be disproved nor affirmed that the age of the father at the time of marriage has an influence upon the vitality of the children; it is certain, however, that if any influence of that kind exists it is much less intense than that exercised by the age of the mother.

There has also been an enquiry as to the effect upon the characters of the offspring exerted by (1) order of birth; (2) difference in age of the parents; and (3) the age of the woman at the first menstruation.

C. Persons who die at a more advanced age have children in greater number and endowed with greater length of life. For some classes of the unfit (mad, consumptives, suicides) it can be proved beyond question that the number of children born is less and their mortality greater than among married people generally. Those who die of heart disease or of cancer show a number of children slightly higher than the general average of married persons; but that can be attributed to the fact that their age at death is greater than the average age at death of married people.

MATERNITY STATISTICS OF THE STATE OF RHODE IS-LAND, STATE CENSUS OF 1905.

(Abstract.)

BY FREDERICK L. HOFFMAN, LL.D., F.S.S.,
STATISTICIAN OF THE PRUDENTIAL INSURANCE COMPANY OF AMERICA.

As a contribution to the practical study of eugenics the decennial maternity statistics of Rhode Island are of exceptional interest and importance.

In 1905, of 36,766 native-born married women 26,329 (71.6%) were mothers, and 10,477 (28.4%) childless. Of 32,960 foreign-born married women 27,207 (82.5%) were mothers, and 5,753 (17.5%) childless. Contrasting these percentages, the fact requires only to be stated to emphasize its profound and far-reaching social as well as political significance.

Considered with reference to religious belief, 72.7% of Protestant and 80.3% of Roman Catholic married women were mothers. Of married women of Jewish faith 88.0% were mothers.

At ages 25-34, the proportion of native-born mothers having only one child was 35.1%, against 22.6% for the foreign-born; the proportion of mothers having from six to ten children was 6.8% for the native-born, against 12.9% for the foreign-born. At all ages a similar disproportion is apparent.

Vastly more important than the multitude of general social and economic facts are these statistics of what, for want of a better term, may be called *human production*, and which disclose what must be considered the most alarming tendency in American life. Granting that excessively large families are not desirable, at least from an economic point of view, it cannot be questioned that the diminution in the average size of the family, and the increase in the proportion of childless families among the native-born stock is evidence of physical deterioration, and must have a lasting and injurious effect on national life and character.

SECTION IV.

MEDICINE AND EUGENICS.
THE PROPHYLAXIS OF HEREDITARY SYPHILIS AND ITS EUGENIC EFFECT.

(Abstract.)

BY DR. H. HALLOPEAU.

Syphilis is strongly *dysgenic*; it causes the production of profoundly damaged children; in preventing it the physician co-operates effectively with eugenic action. In order to prevent the propagation of this disease we must have recourse to *administrative prophylaxis, prophylaxis by persuasion*, and *prophylaxis by medical measures*.

Administrative prophylaxis must act especially by multiplying gratuitous consultations and in securing, as far as possible, hospital treatment for persons affected by transmissible lesions, especially for prostitutes.

To the physician belongs the duty of acting by *persuasion* in pointing out to syphilitics that they have no right to have children so long as they are liable to transmit their disease to their offspring.

We must abort syphilis if it is in the stage of primary invasion: this invasion is not, as was believed until recently, confined to the chancre and its accompanying swellings; it includes all the intermediate stage; in order to destroy the tripanosomes we must use repeated injections of *benzosulfoneparaminophenylarsinate of soda*, commonly known as *hectine* (Mouneyrat), the only specific medicament which is well borne locally.

Results similar to those we have just shown are obtained by making, in a given region, two or three injections of salvarsan. However, the comparison between the two medications is altogether in favour of that by hectine. Indeed, experience proves that the secondary generalization is noticeably more frequent after injections of salvarsan, and, besides, these are far from being always painless. We have made known to the Académie of Medicine a case in which, within 48 hours, they caused the death of a young man in good health. Several similar cases have since been notified, particularly by Dr. Gaucher. Confidently believing in the axiom "Primo non nocere," we explicitly declare ourselves adversaries of a practice which brings such accidents in its train.

In the secondary stage, we must have recourse simultaneously to various specific agents.

Procreation may be permitted when six months after the abortive treatment Wasserman's reaction, after several trials, has given uniformly negative results.

The physician thus accomplishes a profoundly eugenic work in favouring and accelerating the production of unspoilt children.

THE EFFECT OF ALCOHOL ON THE GERM-PLASM.

(THE NEW ALCOHOL LEGISLATION IN NORWAY.)

(Abstract.)

BY DR. ALFRED MJOËN.

The injurious effect of alcohol depends not only upon the amount taken, but also upon other factors, as, *e.g.*, upon its dilution, and upon the kind of nourishment taken with it. There can be no doubt that alcohol under a certain percentage neither injures nor can injure either the somatic cells, or what is more important for race-hygiene, the germ cells. And, on the other hand, it must be regarded as proved that alcohol over a certain percentage is injurious to the quality of the offspring, not alone where the mother drinks (influence upon the embryo), but also where the father alone is a drinker (destruction of the germ). The latest investigations in this field confirm this assumption.

There is, it is true, a middle class of beverages whose influence upon the germ-plasm (posterity) has not been established, or can be established at all. As a general rule, one may lay down the rule: *The injurious effect of an alcoholic beverage upon individuals or race increases from a certain percentage progressively with its increasing contents of alcohol.*

Therefore, I propose to divide alcoholic liquors into classes, and to deal with them according to the amount of their contents of alcohol, *i.e.*, according to their injuriousness.

All casks, bottles, etc., coming into the market are to be furnished with the class-mark (*e.g.*, I., II., III., branded upon the cord).

For example, in the case of beer, the first class (under $2^1/_4$%), shall be obtainable everywhere. For this class there will be claimed, besides a reduction of duty, also a facility for sale and some concessions. Class I. (up to $2^1/_4$%) will be charged with 2 ore; Class II. ($2^1/_4 - 3^3/_4$%) with 8 ore; and Class III. ($3^3/_4 - 5$%) with 15-16 ore per litre. Beer over 5% or $5^1/_2$% will be prohibited([3]).

---

[3] This proposal was favourably received by the Norwegian minister Knudsen, and brought before the Storthing as a Government measure. The proposal has been accepted as part of the election programme of the Radicals, the Socialist Democrats, and all total abstinence organisations.

The class system permits of a simple, cheap, and practicable control, and, indeed, a control which is not confined to the brewery or to any single stage of preparation, but which follows the article over the whole country from its origin to its consumption. When alcoholic drinks are marked with their class and placed under State control, the consumers will themselves easily exercise the control. And the public will gradually become accustomed to form an opinion upon the influence of the various articles upon the working capacity and the health, not only of the individual, but also of the family and the race. State and country authorities will, with State-controlled classes, more easily see justice done on all sides. This last advantage will, naturally, only avail in those lands where the permission to sell alcoholic liquors is vested in the local authorities. The progressive class system will also give the State, the municipalities, and also private labour organisations an opportunity to support those restaurants and inns which supply nothing but pure and harmless liquors, and consumption will undergo a slow and gradual change to the lightest drinks.

At the present time the lightest kinds of beer are too heavily taxed in comparison with the heaviest kinds, and the latter in turn are too heavily taxed in comparison with brandy. From the point of view of race-hygiene, the fight must be directed especially against the fourth and most dangerous class, namely, all kinds of brandy (prohibition or Ivan Bratt's system), as well as against the mixed wines, which are so often adulterated and injurious.

ALCOHOLISM AND DEGENERACY.

Statistics from the Central Bureau for the Management of the Insane of Paris and the Department of the Seine from 1867 to 1912.

(Abstract.)

BY M. MAGNAN,
CHIEF PHYSICIAN TO THE CENTRAL BUREAU, MEMBER OF THE ACADEMY OF MEDICINE,
AND DR. FILLASSIER.

From 1869 to 1912 the number of sick persons received at the Central Bureau of the St. Anne Asylum has gone on steadily increasing: occasionally signs of a falling off are noticed, quickly compensated by the number of entries for the following years.

Among these patients a great number are driven to the asylum by the abuse of alcoholic drinks. Some of these are simple alcoholics, *i.e.*, those who owe their insanity entirely to excessive drinking; the others make up the numerous group of degenerates, who are for the most part descendants of alcoholics, and on whom fall all the forms of physical, intellectual, and moral degradation.

For these last, alcohol has been but the touch of the trigger which has put in action their disposition towards insanity; the attack of mania, when past, leaves revealed psychic troubles, which, but for the turning of the balance by alcohol, would have remained in the latent condition, but which, once developed, remain often for a much longer time; so we see the increase in the number of these patients—occasional drunkards—keeping pace with that of chronic alcoholics.

These will specially call forth the interest of the members of the Eugenic Congress. From the clinical point of view they exhibit great importance; for showing as they do all the episodic syndromes of degeneracy, all the mental forms of it may be seen—maniacal, melancholic, idiotic: insanities polymorphous or systematic, fixed ideas, monomanias connected with words or numbers, every sort of phobia, obsession, impulse, and symptomatic manifestation of great importance. When their objective lies in sexual perversion, theft, arson, murder, etc., these various states raise the most delicate questions whether from the point of view of philosophy, psychology, sociology, or forensic medicine.

This class of society, in the grip of this poison, is unfortunately not sterile; their miserable descendants come to dock in the asylum; so much so that if we mass together the various elements, if we add the unfortunates permanently disabled, such as epileptics, and the increasing crowd of feeble-minded, idiotic, tuberculous children, the mind recoils aghast at the gravity of the danger. The necessity of an implacable war against alcoholism, which crowds our asylums, our hospitals, and our homes with insane persons, and sends a constant stream to our prisons and reformatories—such a war must be the principal aim of the Eugenics Congress.

For long the evil genius of mankind, alcoholism has to-day laid its clutch on women, and the admission figures now show their numbers on the increase every year.

Such are the lessons which may be learnt from the report of Magnan and Fillassier.

EUGENICS AND OBSTETRICS.

(Abstract.)

BY DR. AGNES BLUHM,
BERLIN.

1. Among the agencies under social control which impair the racial qualities of future generations, an important place is taken by the Science of Medicine, especially by Obstetrics. For the increase of obstetrics increases the incapacity for bearing children of future generations.

2. The great difference in the capacity for bearing children between the primitive and civilized races depends only in part on the lessened fitness of the latter due to the increase of skilled assistance.

3. Incapacity for bearing children can be acquired; it develops, however, abundantly on the grounds of a congenital predisposition.

4. In so far as the latter is the case, obstetrics contributes towards the diffusion of this incapacity.

5. The most serious obstacles to delivery are effected by deformities of the pelvis, in at least 90% of which heredity plays a part. In this connection, rickets, the predisposition to which is inherited, takes the foremost place.

6. German medical statistics make it appear probable that incapacity to bear children is on the increase.

7. Medical help in childbirth brings, undoubtedly, numerical advantage to the race, but it endangers the quality of the race in other ways than through the fostering of unfitness for bearing.

8. The danger of the increase of incapacity for bearing through the increase of assistance in childbirth can be combatted:—

(*a*) Through the renunciation of descendants by women unfitted to bear children.

(*b*) Through an energetic campaign against rickets, to which only the predisposition can be inherited.

(*c*) Through the permeation of obstetrics with the spirit of eugenics, so that the obstetrician no longer proceeds according to a settled rule (living mother and living child), but in each separate case takes into consideration the interests of the race.

HEREDITY AND EUGENICS IN RELATION TO INSANITY.

(Abstract.)

BY F. W. MOTT, M.D., F.R.S.,
*PHYSICIAN TO CHARING CROSS HOSPITAL AND PATHOLOGIST
TO THE LONDON COUNTY ASYLUMS.*

What is insanity? Every case of insanity is a biological problem, the solution of which depends upon a knowledge of what a man was born with—Nature—and what has happened after birth—Nurture. The increase of registered insanity in London; the causes of the increase. (1) The standard of insanity has been raised. (2) The increase of accommodation for reception of the insane. The diminishing death rate in asylums causing a progressive accumulation. The diminished number of recoveries. (3) The large proportion of old people admitted to asylums formerly in the infirmaries.

Nurture.—The correlation of pauperism, insanity and feeble-mindedness, alcohol, syphilis, and tuberculosis in relation to insanity and feeble-mindedness. Congenital mental deficiency as distinguished from hereditary mental deficiency. Chronic poisoning of the blood by these agencies in relation to a lowered specific vitality of the germ cells. Environment in relation to mental energy and will power.

Nature.—The study of pedigrees in hospital and asylum patients showing the importance of heredity in nervous and mental diseases. The nature of the neuropathic tendency; its transmission in different forms of nervous and mental disease in successive generations. Its latency and re-appearance in stocks. Relation of neurasthenia to the neuropathic taint. Conclusions arrived at in relation to heredity and insanity from a study by a card system of 3,118 related persons who are at present, or who have been, in the London County asylums. Among the 20,000 inmates at present resident, 715 are so closely related as parents and offspring or brothers and sisters. Nature is always trying to end or mend a degenerate stock if left to itself. Analysis of data regarding first attack of insanity in 464 parents and their 508 offspring; the signal tendency to the occurrence of the disease in a more intense form and at an earlier age in the offspring. This "antedating" or "anticipation" in relation to Nature's process of elimination of the unfit. Nearly 50 per cent. of the offspring affected 20 years earlier than the parent. The same found in uncles and aunts with nephews and nieces, only not nearly so marked. Seeing that the unfit are at present able to survive; does nature end or mend degenerate stocks, or have the lines of neuropathic inheritance only been partially cut off by this tendency to "anticipation"? What we want to know is: What is the fate of all the offspring of an insane parent or parents; for there are a great many facts which show that a disease may be latent and re-appear in a stock when the conditions of mating or environment are unfavourable? A collection of pedigrees is required which will prove conclusively that the offspring of insane parents, who are free from the insane manifestations during adolescence, will breed children who will not become insane. Supposing it were shown that cases discharged as recovered had the seeds of insanity, by the fact that their progeny were feeble-minded, epileptic, or insane, it would be a clear indication of taking measures to prevent them handing on the disease. Recurrent insanity—the birth of children in the sane intervals. Analysis of pedigrees with a dual neuropathic inheritance of maternal and paternal stocks compared with single neuropathic inheritance. Conclusion that a child born of neuropathic inheritance in both ancestral stocks stands, on an average, the chance of being insane four times as great as when only one stock is affected. Are there any types of insanity especially liable to be transmitted in the same form or another form? The prediction of the racial value of an individual inheritance can only be predicted by a study of what a man was born with—Nature, and what happened after birth—Nurture.

THE PLACE OF EUGENICS IN THE MEDICAL CURRICULUM.

(Abstract.)

BY H. E. JORDAN,
CHAIRMAN OF THE EUGENICS SECTION OF THE AMERICAN ASSOCIATION FOR THE STUDY AND PREVENTION OF INFANT MORTALITY.

The Science of Eugenics deserves a place in the medical curriculum for three reasons. Firstly: Medicine is fast becoming a science of the prevention of weakness and morbidity; their permanent not temporary cure, their racial eradication rather than their personal palliation. Eugenic conduct is undeniably a factor in attaining the speedy achievement of the end of racial health. Eugenics, embracing genetics, is thus one of the important disciplines among the future medical sciences. The coming physician must have adequate training in matters relating to heredity and Eugenics. Secondly: as the general population becomes better educated in matters of personal and racial health and hygiene it will more and more demand advice regarding the prevention of weakness in themselves and their offspring. The physicians are logically the men who must give it. Thirdly: physicians will be more efficient public servants if they approach their work with the Eugenic outlook on life.

Instruction in Eugenics, in the form of a number of special lectures on the subject, is already given in some of our medical schools. This indicates at least that the need is felt and the importance of such knowledge to the best physician recognised. Since not all of the better medical schools give such courses, however, we may infer that there are obstacles in the way. What is the nature of these?

One such may be the lack of adequate preparation on the part of the students in the fundamentals of biology to properly comprehend the import and application of Eugenic facts. This obstacle is speedily being removed; for considerable biological training is already a medical course prerequisite. But there may be a lack of properly prepared teachers to present this subject to even properly prepared medical students. This obstacle is also fast disappearing. Once the demand for this kind of help is voiced, there will appear properly trained teachers to instruct physicians.

Another obstacle may be raised by short-sighted and self-seeking physicians, for whom less illness and weakness may mean less work and a reduced income.

But this is, perhaps, only a relatively very small factor in, and also only a passing phase of, the opposition, and will soon correct itself.

The most encouraging prospect for this new scheme of activity is the deep interest shown by young medical students in matters of heredity and Eugenics.

A HEALTHY SANE FAMILY SHOWING LONGEVITY IN CAT-ALONIA.

(Abstract.)

BY PROFESSOR I. VALENTI VIVO.

I. A healthy family showing longevity in Catalonia: the greater part of them died over 60 years of age from acute sickness. All belonged to the districts of Barcelona and Gerona. A record of their ability in medical science, art and agriculture, their average fertility.

II. Communication on Biometrika: Licentiates in medical science, 50 scholars, 1910: 70 in 1912. Dates: Cephalic index, stature, span, dynamometer, age, district.

SOME REMARKS ON BACKWARD CHILDREN.

(Abstract.)

BY DR. RAOUL DUPUY.

When we speak of a backward child, we mean any subject which is arrested or retarded more or less completely in its bodily, psychical, and sensorial evolution, in consequence of congenital and acquired lesions, or simply in consequence of physiological troubles, which concern, either at the same or a different time, the brain and the glands of internal secretion (the thyroid, the hypophysis, the suprarenals, and the genital glands). The cerebral lesions, practically incurable in the present state of science, produce "atropic backwardness" the functional troubles of the brain, or those caused by the glands of internal secretion, which can be modified by "combined organotherapy" produce dystrophic backwardness. We also, however, find mixed types, half of the one and half of the other, which are similarly susceptible of improvement. The number, and above all the variety of the types of dystrophic backwardness, makes a general classification of them impossible. The study of their bodily, psychical and sensorial anomalies proves that in most of the manifestations of backwardness and immaturity, these children present perversions of evolution which have a common bearing on the development of body, mind and spirit. Although apparently different from one another, these backward persons, whether the mischief be corporal, psychical or sensorial, show pathological peculiarities, which prove that the cause of their various dystrophies have a similar origin, and that they often arise from defective function of the sympathic system which appears to be brought into action by the internal glands. The backward children consist of intoxicated, under-grown or anæmic persons, who, besides, suffer from retention of substances, which ought normally to be eliminated, chiefly the chlorides and phosphates (in cases of apathy) or the hyper excretion of the same substances (in cases of instability). Moreover, the combined organotherapy ought to be considered as a "perfect touchstone" of dystrophy, and if applied according to certain rules, it gives results which are more complete and more certain than thyroid organotherapy by itself. It goes without saying that a special training is necessary for the intellectual "backwards"; but before any attempt at education, it is necessary to treat their bodily deficiencies, and to place them in the special schools with the boarding system, where they will be under the eye both of the doctor and of the teacher.

Lector House believes that a society develops through a two-fold approach of continuous learning and adaptation, which is derived from the study of classic literary works spread across the historic timeline of literature records. Therefore, we aim at reviving, repairing and redeveloping all those inaccessible or damaged but historically as well as culturally important literature across subjects so that the future generations may have an opportunity to study and learn from past works to embark upon a journey of creating a better future.

This book is a result of an effort made by Lector House towards making a contribution to the preservation and repair of original ancient works which might hold historical significance to the approach of continuous learning across subjects.

HAPPY READING & LEARNING!

LECTOR HOUSE LLP
E-MAIL: lectorpublishing@gmail.com